# ISIS

## wants to kill you

# A concise history of the world's most terrifying organization

David Stansfield

Edited by Allen Waldman

Volume One of a series of short
illustrated books about terrorism

David Stansfield

ISIS wants to kill you/David Stansfield
Edited by Allen Waldman

ISBN-13: 978-1515126638
ISBN-10: 1515126633

SULBY HALL
PUBLISHERS

USA: PO Box 6867
Malibu CA 90264

Canada: 28 Duncannon Drive,
Toronto ON M5P 2M1

www.sulbyhall.com
and at
www.davidstansfield.com

*Cover design by David Stansfield & Denise Boiteau*

Printed in the United States of America

David Stansfield is an Arabic scholar, who has lived in many parts of the Middle East with different Arab families. He graduated from Durham University with First Class Honors (summa cum laude) in Arabic Studies, and continued studying the language and the culture at the universities of Cambridge, Paris and Toronto, whereupon he was recruited by MI6, the British equivalent of the CIA.

David later went on to write and produce the 14-part TVOntario/Encyclopedia Britannica television series: "The Middle East," which was selected for consideration for an Academy Award in the best educational documentary category.

David Stansfield

*These are the worst people on earth. They openly, proudly crucify enemies, enslave women, and murder men en masse. These are not the usual bad guys out for land, plunder, or power. These are primitive cultists who celebrate slaughter, glory in bloodlust, and slit the throats of innocents as a kind of sacrament.*

Charles Krauthammer, National Review Online, August 21, 2014

David Stansfield

# TABLE OF CONTENTS

David Stansfield

It began with the announcements, plastered all over town.

Every head of every household was to bring all the females in his care to headquarters to be used as sex slaves by the "liberators." Those who refused were visited by a party of fighters. First, they brutalized, then tortured, and ultimately shot the master of the house, along with every other male, young or old, in his family. Then they gang raped all the females in his family, young or old. If any girl or woman resisted, they beat her with the butts of their guns until she was close to death. Then they gang raped her all over again.

Then they turned off the oil. It wasn't difficult, given that they controlled the countries that possessed two-thirds of all the oil in the world.

Finally, they used the tunnel. There were many such tunnels, but this one was only 600 yards long, and straight as a die, funneling cocaine and heroin and desperate human beings – and now the nuclear device – from Tijuana to Otay Mesa, a suburb of San Diego, where they pushed the button.

And that was the end.

Could this happen here?

Yes.

Their name is ISIS and they are planning to do all this and a great deal more in the name of God.

# 1. The caliphate

So what on earth is ISIS? Let's start with the name itself. ISIS stands for the Islamic State of Iraq and Syria. It is also referred to in English as ISL, which stands for the Islamic State of the Levant. "Levant" is the French for "rising," as in the place where the sun rises, the Eastern end of the Mediterranean, which stretches from Israel and Palestine to Iraq.

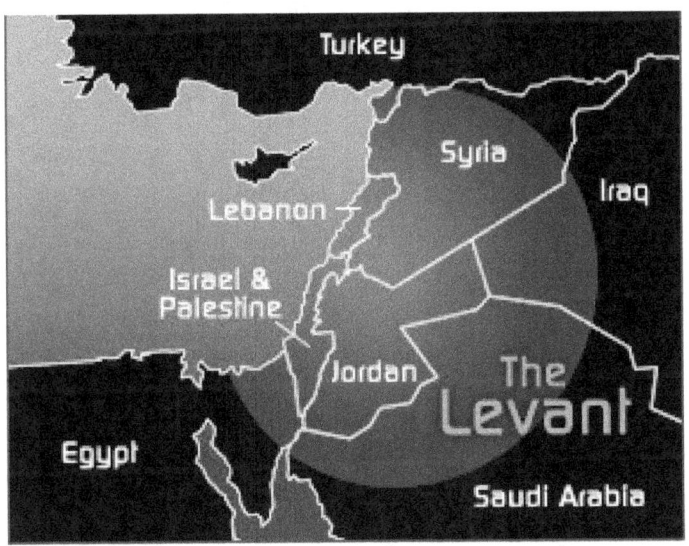

But the Arabic name of this organization gives much more meaning than the English acronym ISIS. It is الدولة الإسلامية في العراق والشام *ad-dawlat al-islamiyya fi'l-'iraq wa'sh-sham*, reduced in Arabic to the acronym *Da'ish:* "The Islamic State in Iraq and *Sham.*"

The word *Sham* is the key; it resonates in the Arabic-speaker's mind on multiple levels. What does it mean?

Well, one thing it does NOT mean is the truncated Syria that was created by the French in 1922. Rather, it means the "North," the "Greater Syria" that encompasses, not only the artificial states the British and the French carved out of the Ottoman Empire after World War One: Syria, Iraq, Lebanon, Jordan, Palestine and subsequently Israel, but also Cyprus and part of southern Turkey.

For most of the last four thousand five hundred years, nearly all of these phony modern states were one, not only under the empires of the Ottomans, the Arabs, the Byzantines, the Romans, the Greeks and the Persians, but also under the AsSYRIAns, and even more ancient civilizations before them, dating all the way back to 2,500 B.C.

Sham's roots run very deep – and dangerously –

indeed, as we shall see.

However, ISIS's ambitions stretch a lot farther afield than *Sham*. Its ultimate goal is to gain control not only of the entire Middle East from Morocco to Iran...

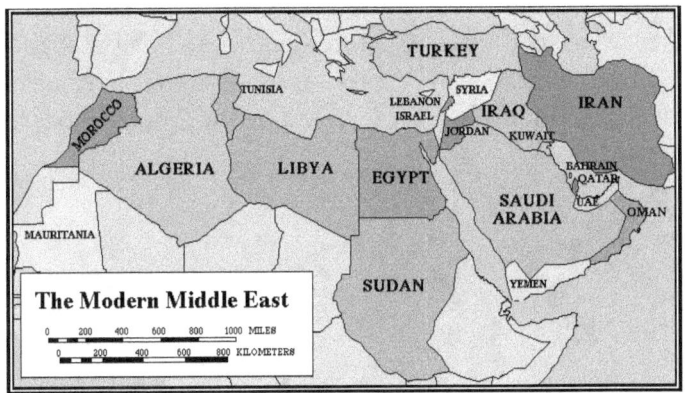

...but of the entire Islamic world, which includes a score of African countries, numerous parts of Russia, plus Albania, Bosnia, Kosovo Ajerbaijan, Kazakhstan, Tajkistan, Turkmanistan, Uzbekistan, Afghanistan, Pakistan, Bangladesh, Malaysia and Indonesia.

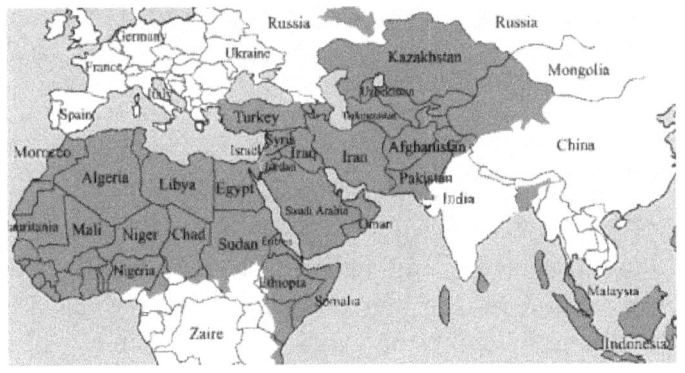

Why is ISIS doing this? Because its members want to set up what they call a "caliphate" over this entire world. No small feat, since this Islamic world numbers 1.6 billion people; the planet's second largest religion after Christianity, which weighs in at 2.2 billion.

What is a caliphate? To answer that we have to go back over fourteen hundred years to 610 A.D. and a cave near the city of Mecca in what is now Saudi Arabia, where an Arab man by the name of Muhammad has just been visited by the Angel Gabriel.

Gabriel asks Muhammad to recite a series of verses, which he assures him come directly from God.

Over the next twenty-two years, Gabriel is to visit Muhammad again and again with more and more verses from God for him to recite, all of which are subsequently to be chunked together into "The "Recitation," *al-qur'ān*, or Koran as we mangle it.

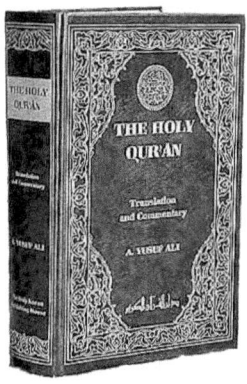

Several verses of the *Qur'ān* stand out from the rest because they contain the first ever appearances of the word *Muslim*. Here's an example:

> *We are supporters of God. We have believed in God and testify that we are Muslims* [i.e., that we are submitting to Him].

All of today's 1.6 billion Muslims have to believe that the period between 610 and 632 when Muhammad received God's revelations represents the one and only period during which God spoke to man since the universe began.

This is the basis of Islam itself, the foundation of the faith of every Muslim. Precisely because God only spoke to Muhammad, and precisely because He spoke in Arabic, all Muslims have to believe every word of the following Arabic sentence:

# لا إله إلا الله محمد رسول الله

*lā 'ilāha 'illā-llāh, muḥammadun rasūlu-llāh*
There is no god but God,
Muhammad is the messenger of God

In fact, that's all you have to say to become a Muslim in the first place. Try it: *lā 'ilāha 'illā-llāh, muḥammadun rasūlu-llāh*

Congratulations, you're a Muslim.

Now back to the caliphate and what it means.

Muhammad may have been the only man who ever lived whom God contacted directly, but even he couldn't live for ever. As founder of the new religion of Islam, he was eventually able to recruit enough of his fellow desert Arabs to unite most of Arabia into a single religious entity under Islam. But then in early June, 632 A.D., the Messenger fell ill with a fever and died.

The immediate question was, who would be Muhammad's successor? Or as they say in Arabic, his *khalīfah*, his caliph? Who would be the man to rule over the Messenger's succession, his *khilāfa*, his caliphate?

As it happened, the majority of the followers of Muhammad elected his father-in-law and close companion, Abu Bakr, to be Islam's first caliph.

Leap forward in history to Iraq in 2014 and the self-appointed leader of ISIS, Ibrahim Ali al-Badri al-Samarrai as he declares himself Islam's latest caliph, conveniently changing his name to *Abu Bakr* al-Baghdadi in the process...

...as he announces ISIS's goal of taking over the world.

## 2. Origins

Where did ISIS come from? The short answer is, it came from al-Qaeda...

...Arabic for "database," which our very own CIA had set up to keep track of the *mujahideen* led by a Saudi by the name of Osama bin Ladin with the aim of kicking the Soviet Army out of Afghanistan.

The whole exercise was a great success and the Soviets were indeed eventually pushed out of that country in 1989 thanks in large part to the *jihad* waged by Osama and his men and our splendid database.

Washington apparently never dreamed that once the Soviets had withdrawn, Osama's "al-Qaeda the database" would morph into "al-Qaeda the terrorist movement," which would promptly turn its attention to attacking the West. But this is exactly what happened after Osama and some of his top associates met in a suburb of Peshawar, Pakistan to discuss the possibility of launching a global jihad now that the Soviets were out of the picture.

Fast-forward to 2001 and al-Qaeda's 9/11 attack on the Twin Towers...

...and then to our 2003 response, which was not to invade al-Qaeda's headquarters in Pakistan to obliterate this new enemy, but to invade Iraq, the one place everyone knew did *not* harbor al-Qaeda since its secular ruler and our former ally, and Donald Rumsfeld's "good friend," Saddam Hussein, was Osama's sworn enemy.

Fast-forward again to 2007 as the raging civil war our calamitous invasion of Iraq had triggered continued to tear the country apart and inadvertently provoke exactly the opposite of what it set out achieve by promoting the gradual emergence of "Al-Qaeda in Iraq."

Final fast-forward to 2013 as al-Qaeda in Iraq – now based in both Syria and Iraq – rebrands itself as something much, much worse: the Islamic State in Iraq and *Sham*, or ISIS.

Guess what both al-Qaeda and ISIS have written on their flags:

لا إله إلا الله محمد رسول الله

*lā ʾilāha ʾillā-llāh, muḥammadun rasūlu-llāh*
There is no god but God,
Muhammad is the messenger of God

## 3. Fighters

As of early 2015, the ISIS army totaled almost a quarter of a million fighters and support personnel. Where did all these people come from? Who are all these great warriors?

Well, to start with they are all Sunnis. What's a Sunni? To answer that, we have to dive back into history again and the moment when most of Muhammad's followers elected his father-in-law, Abu Bakr, to be Islam's first Caliph. Trouble is, some of the Prophet's followers didn't agree and thought that Muhammad's son-in-law, Ali, should be the first Caliph. Oh, those pesky in-laws – and the family squabbles they were going to lead to.

Because the pro-Abu Bakr supporters called themselves *ahl as-sunnah*, the people of the tradition (of Muhammad), they became known as the Sunnis. The Ali supporters, on the other hand, called themselves *shī'atu 'Alī,* the party of Ali, so they became known as the Shia or the Shiites.

Today, about 85% of Muslims are Sunni and 15% are Shia, distributed across the Middle East like this:

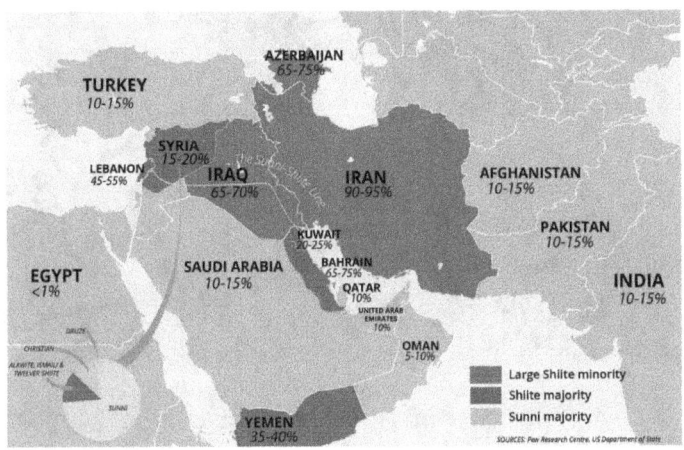

We see that 65-70% of Iraqis are Shia and 30-35% are Sunni. But in spite of their minority status, up until the U.S. invasion, the Sunnis controlled the country under the leadership of the Sunni President Saddam Hussein, who murdered 60,000 to 100,000 Shiites after one of their uprisings against his regime.

Three years after we'd toppled Saddam, following our 2003 invasion of Iraq...

...we replaced him with a Shiite Prime Minister, Noury al-Maliki, who set about persecuting the Sunnis almost as ruthlessly as Saddam had persecuted the Shia. This Sunni poster of the Prime Minister labels him, "Hypocrite, liar, swindler, sectarian, thief, twister."

To make matters worse – in fact, much, much worse – shortly after our invasion of the country we disbanded the overwhelmingly Sunni Iraqi army, laying off almost 500,000 military and civilian personnel, tens of thousands of whom ended up in ISIS out of desperation, unable to resist the monthly salary of $400 dollars, free housing, ISIS-approved schooling for children and round-the-clock access to sex slaves. Today it is estimated that at least 25 of ISIS's top 40 leaders once served in the Iraqi military.

In addition to all this, more than 20,000 fighters have flocked to join ISIS from all over the world:

## FOREIGN FIGHTERS IN IRAQ/SYRIA
Top 10 countries of origin (Total numbers)

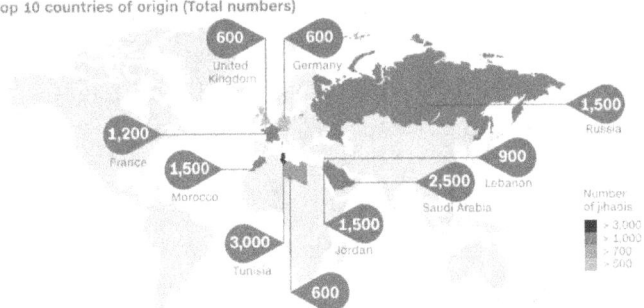

600 — United Kingdom
600 — Germany
1,500 — Russia
1,200 — France
1,500 — Morocco
900 — Lebanon
2,500 — Saudi Arabia
1,500 — Jordan
3,000 — Tunisia
600 — Libya

Number of jihadis
> 3,900
> 1,000
> 700
> 500

SOURCES: International Centre for the Study of Radicalisation and Political Violence; Soufan Group; Pew Research Center

## 4. Women

Are all the nearly 250,000 ISIS fighters and supporters men? No, in fact about 10% of them are women, who like their male counterparts, come mainly from the Middle East, but also from many foreign countries all over the world (80% of Muslims live outside of the Middle East and North Africa.).

Why are all these women shrouded from head to foot in those burkas? Where is it written in the Koran that they should dress in this ridiculous fashion? Nowhere. In fact, the only mention of any sort of covering at all for women in the 600-odd pages of the Holy Book is in Chapter 24, Verse 31:

> *And say to the believing women, that they cast down their eyes and* guard their private parts, *and reveal not their adornment save such as is outward; and let them cast their veils over their* bosoms, *and not reveal their adornment*

*save to their husbands, or their fathers, or their
husbands' fathers, or their sons, or their
husbands' sons, or their brothers, or their
brothers' sons...*

In other words, don't go out in public topless and bottomless. An edict that is obeyed even on the licentious streets of America last time we checked.

But there is another aspect of ISIS's treatment of women that is not so funny. This brave fighter is announcing his marriage to a terrified seven-year old girl – a sex slave, in other words – permitted by Islam according to ISIS because she is an "unbeliever."

What does the Koran have to say about slavery and the treatment of women? In verse 75 of the chapter, entitled "The Women," God says:

*What is wrong with you, that you do not fight in the way of God, and for the oppressed men, women, and children who say, "Our Lord, bring us forth from this town whose people are evildoers and appoint for us a protector from You, and appoint for us from You a helper."*

See also verse 12 of the chapter called "The Land," *al-balad:*

*And what will show you what the obstacle is?, the freeing of a slave, or to give food on a day of hunger.*

As 126 outraged Muslim scholars from all over the world (speaking for the 99.9% of Muslims who do NOT support ISIS) wrote to Abu Bakr al-Baghdadi. "You have made children engage in war and killing. Some are taking up arms and others are playing with the severed heads of your victims. Some children have been thrown into the fray of combat and are killing and being killed. In your schools some children are tortured and coerced into doing your bidding and others are being executed. These are crimes against innocents who are so young they are not even morally accountable."

The scholars went on to make three important points:

- "The re-introduction of slavery is forbidden in Islam. It was abolished by universal consensus."
- "It is forbidden in Islam to deny women their rights."

- "It is forbidden in Islam to deny children their rights."

But what has ISIS done over the past year? What haven't they done?

Just to give one typical example: the Kurdish Yazidis of Iraq. These defenseless people were subjected to a terrifying avalanche of horrors: the exile of some 60,000 of them...

...the massacre of over 5,000 male civilians...

...and the enslavement of thousands of Yazidi women, girls and small boys...

...many of the females being used as sex slaves or put on sale at public auctions...

For a bunch of people who keep bragging about what devout Muslims they are, the ISIS gang certainly don't know much about their Holy Book. Almost everything they have done has not been in the name of the true Koran, any more than it has been in the name of the over 1.5 billion true Muslims, who condemn their horrific barbarism and insane ideology.

## 5. Punishments

January, 2015: ISIS published a penal code listing crimes punishable by flogging, amputation, beheading, stoning and crucifixion, along with a vow to ensure the code is rigorously enforced in areas currently under its control in Syria and Iraq.

Here are the main crimes and their punishments:

*One.* Blasphemy against God: Death.

*Two.* Blasphemy against the Prophet Muhammad: Death – even if the accuser repents.

*Three.* Blasphemy against Islam: Death.

*Four.* Adultery: Stoning until death if the adulterer was married and 100 lashes and exile if he or she was unmarried.

*Five.* Sodomy: Death for the person committing the act, as well as for the one receiving it.

*Six.* Theft: Cutting off the hand.

*Seven*. Drinking alcohol: 80 lashes.

*Eight*. Slandering: 80 lashes.

*Nine*. Spying for the unbelievers: Death by Crucifixion.

*Ten*. Apostasy: Death by Crucifixion.

What does the Koran say about these savage punishments? Nothing. Not a word – with the sole exception of "fornication," which is punishable by flogging with a "hundred stripes," and theft which is only punishable in certain, very limited circumstances, the Holy Book of Islam does not utter a single syllable concerning the other eight punishments.

Finally, we come to the atrocities that have sickened us perhaps more than anything else that ISIS has done to date: the ruthless beheading of Western aid workers and journalists such as James Foley shown here about to have his head cut off by the British-born "Jihadi John."

Now to end this chapter on a happier note: a story about virgins and grapes. ISIS – and other Islamic terrorist organizations – claim that if you are killed in the line of duty as a fighter or a suicide bomber, you will be rewarded with 72 virgins in Heaven.

This belief is based on Chapter 44, Verses 50-54 in the Koran:

> *Surely the God-fearing shall be in a station secure among gardens and fountains, robed in silk and brocade, set face to face. Even so; and We shall marry them to wide-eyed* houris, *therein calling for every fruit, secure.*

The key word is "*houris,*" which means wide-eyed (i.e. pure, virgin) young ladies. The only trouble is, according to some scholars, this word can also mean "white grapes."

or

# 6. Root causes

How can the ISIS fighters commit such horrendous crimes? How can people become eaten up by so much anger and hate? Are these people all simply psychopaths? Tens of thousands of books and articles and scholarly papers have been written about such monsters and we still don't know the answer.

But we can perhaps get at least part of an explanation for ISIS, if we consider the almost non-stop humiliation the Middle East has been subjected to by the Western Powers over the last 100 years.

Where did this all start?

With World War One.

Let's backtrack a bit to the Ottoman/Turkish Empire that ruled almost all of the Middle East for some four hundred years. Four centuries of relative peace in this region compared to the almost nonstop wars that were going on in Europe during this same period.

Then came the Great War when the Ottoman Turks made the catastrophic mistake of siding with the Germans and all Hell broke loose as the "Sick Man of Europe" lay on his death bed and the British and the French moved in to pick up the pieces – or, more accurately to split the region up into completely arbitrary pieces.

At its height in the 1500s, the Ottoman Empire controlled all this:

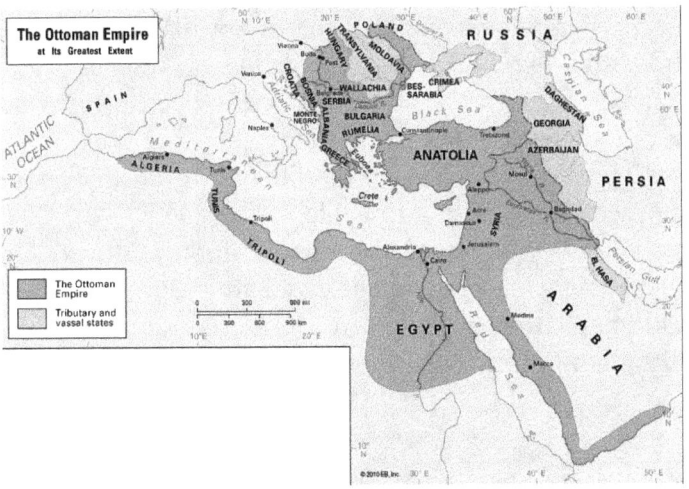

By 1913, after Britain had grabbed Egypt, and France had grabbed all the rest of North Africa, the Ottoman Empire was reduced to this:

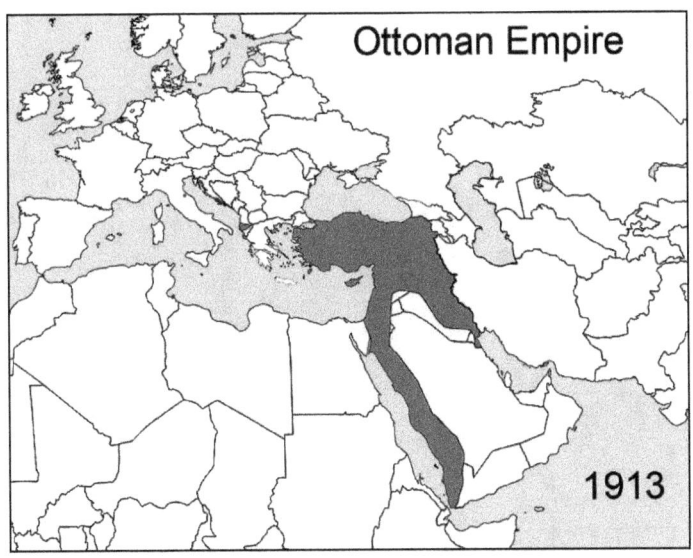

This area encompassed what is now Turkey, most of Iraq and Syria, Palestine, Jordan and western Saudi Arabia. These areas had traditionally been divided up very loosely, with fluid, constantly changing boundaries reflecting the movements of different ethnic, religious and sectarian groups of people.

Then World War One broke out and the British and the French marched in, defeated the German-backed Ottoman Turks and divided up the central part of the Ottoman Empire between them as shown below:

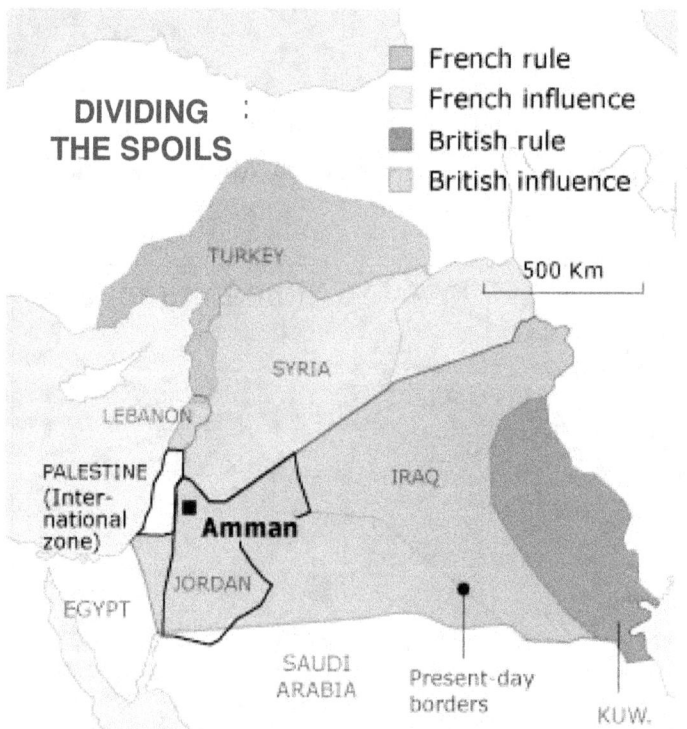

Not surprisingly, this stroke of supreme imperialist arrogance immediately began to wreak havoc among the various groups of people involved as their age-old spiritual space was replaced by the deranged geometry of pencils and rulers drawing dead straight lines through ancestral tribal domains.

On top of that, the British and French colonialists, wanting to keep both the Jews and the Arabs on their side during their battles with the Ottomans, promised one particular part of the region to both peoples. This little pocket of real estate about the size of New Jersey – now named Israel or Palestine, depending which side you're on – has been a problem ever since.

The imperial hubris didn't stop there. One of the wielders of pencil and ruler by the name of Winston Churchill...

...already celebrated for his fondness of liquid lunches, drew a sudden postprandial zigzag in the middle of the Jordanian/Saudi Arabian border that is known to this day as "Churchill's Hiccup." He even boasted that he had created Jordan "with the stroke of a pen, one Sunday afternoon in Cairo."

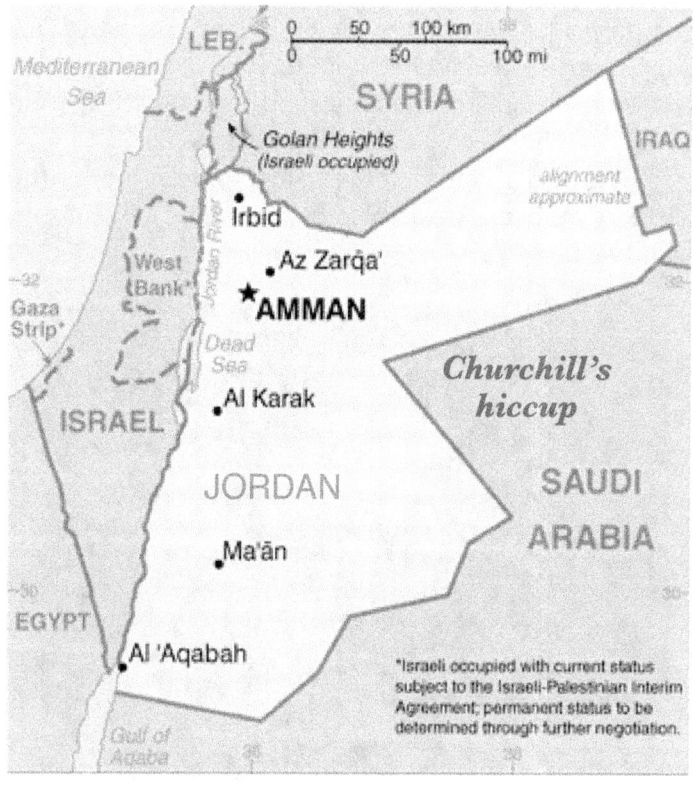

To see your ancient land, which for centuries had been open and free for different groups of people to move about almost wherever they liked, suddenly constricted and carved up as the imperialists' rulers cut straight through your hearts and lives and histories, all but driving you out of your minds; this way lay madness – and fury.

It got worse. Here's a list of the dictatorial regimes that have sprung up in the Middle East in recent years (almost always with our assistance):

- Hosni Mubarak, Egypt
- Mohammad Reza Pahlavi, Iran
- Saddam Hussein, Iraq
- Bashar Al Assad, Syria
- Moammar Gaddafi, Libya
- House of Saud, Saudi Arabia
- Ali Abdullah Saleh, Yemen
- Hamad bin Isa al-Khalifa, Bahrain
- Zine El Abedine Ben Ali, Tunisia
- Jaber al-Ahmad as-Sabah, Kuwait
- Hamad bin Khalifa ath-Thani, Qatar
- Qaboos bin Said as-Said, Oman
- Muhammad bin Rashid al-Maktoum, UAE

A rogues gallery of captains and kings, emirs and sheikhs devoted to amassing the greatest amount of wealth possible, while suppressing – and when necessary, torturing and murdering – their own people when they stepped out of line. More madness and more fury, building and building.

Not to mention the never-healing open wound of the Israel-Palestine conflict.

And finally, what are already proving to be the two last straws – or rather two last civil wars:

*Civil War #1* in Iraq, where the aforementioned U.S. invasion of Iraq – turning Sunni against Shia – has resulted not only in laying waste to this country...

Shock and Awe

...but in laying off half a million Iraqi military and civilian personnel... fury upon fury...

...plus the deaths of at least 600,000 other Iraqis...

...and the internal displacement of an additional million and a half, and the external displacement of four million, the largest ever such tragedy in the Middle East...

That is, until an even greater tragedy was to take place, which brings us to...

*Civil War #2* in Syria, where our protégé, Bashar Al Assad...

...brutally crushed the "Arab Spring" for daring to jump up and be heard, resulting in the laying waste to that country also...

The city that used to be Homs

...and the deaths of nearly a quarter of a million Syrians.

Assad's lavish use of Sarin nerve gas was particularly effective...

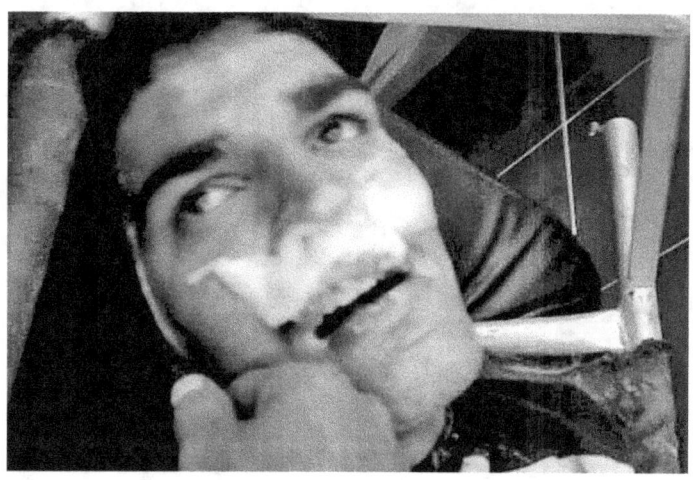

...especially on children.

All this forcing nine million Syrians to flee their homes. That's 40% of the entire population of that country, the equivalent of 127 million Americans becoming homeless.

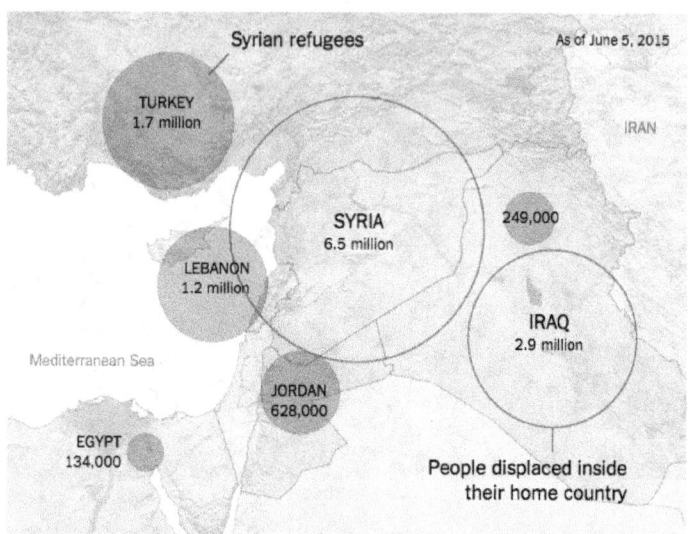

Wouldn't you be just a tiny bit miffed after you and your parents and your grandparents and your great grandparents had experienced a hundred years of all this?

No excuse for the unspeakable brutality of the ISIS fighters, of course, and their lunatic dreams of returning to some mythical 7th century caliphate, but at least the beginning of an explanation for ISIS's appalling behavior.

## 7. The conquest so far

This is what ISIS controls as of June 2015...

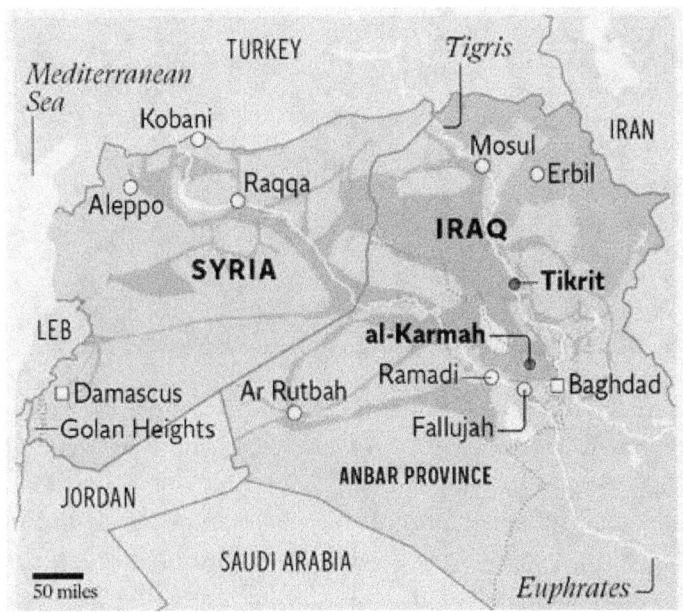

...but note that this territory is expanding very fast indeed. Between August 2014 and January 2015, ISIS-controlled territory in Syria, for example, more than doubled. Across both Iraq and Syria, ISIS now rules over an area the size of Great Britain.

Here are the major cities controlled by ISIS in Iraq and Syria, in one of which, Mosul (population 3 million), 800 ISIS fighters routed two Iraqi Army divisions totaling 30,000 troops.

ISIS is currently within three miles of the Iraqi capital, Baghdad, with only a US Marine Base in their path. And now that ISIS has occupied the Palestinian Yarmouk refugee camp on the outskirts of Damascus, it is within approximately the same distance from the Syria capital. Here the 18,000 inhabitants of Yarmouk line up for emergency food rations...

...after enduring days of a non-stop barrage by pro-Assad forces of IED-style "barrel bombs," large metal containers filled with high explosives, shrapnel, oil or chemicals, dropped from a helicopter or airplane.

ISIS released these pictures of its fighters posing for victory pictures at various locations within the camp.

ISIS has a two-step plan that runs as follows:

*Step One*: Once they have taken Baghdad and Damascus, they will complete their conquest of almost all of Syria and a very large chunk of Iraq...

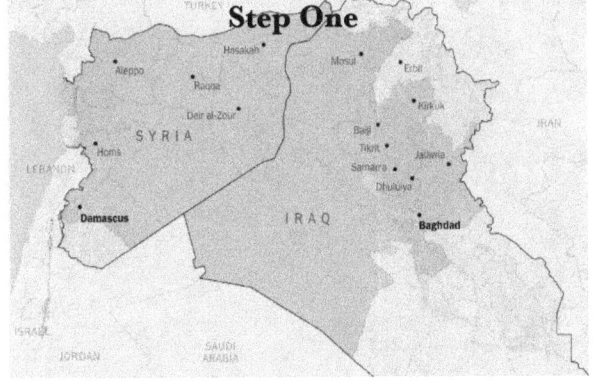

...which will be their interim caliphate while they prepare for:

*Step Two*: taking over the whole world's Muslim population as their ultimate caliphate.

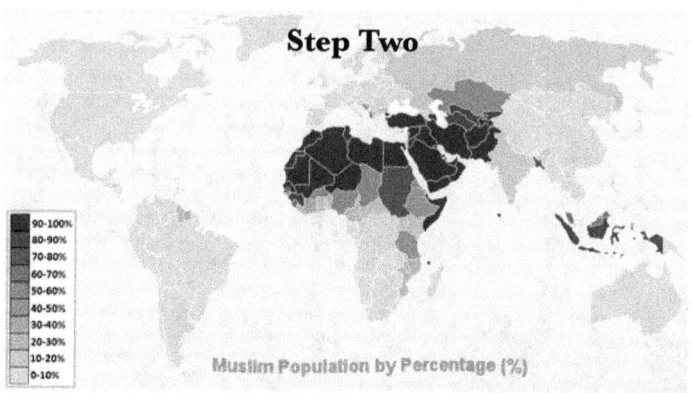

As part of the build up to this, according to the Washington-based Institute for the Study of War, there are now numerous **ISIS** terrorist cells (miniature ISIS organizations) in many different Islamic countries, from North Africa and Nigeria, reaching all across the Middle East to Iran, Georgia, Afghanistan and Pakistan. Just waiting...

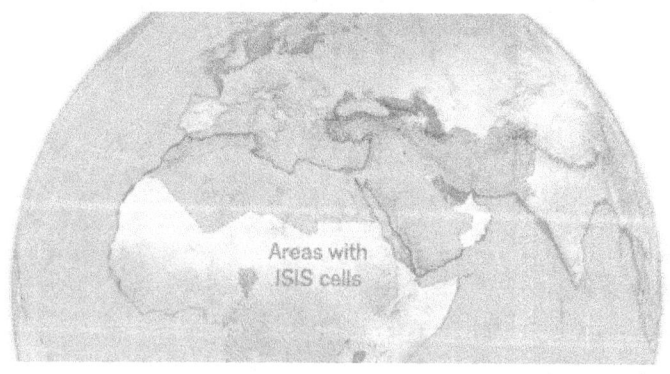

Meanwhile, the number of Iraqis and Syrians under ISIS rule has reached almost seven million.

The rules they have to live by have gone beyond absurd.

All "sisters" have to wear the full-face veil and gloves and refrain from raising their voices in public. Otherwise their husbands or "guardians" will be flogged.

All music and songs are banned in cars, at parties, in shops and in public, as well as photographs of people in shop windows, cigarettes, hookah pipes, t-shirts with English writing on them, men's trousers touching the ground, playing cards and going on picnics because this is "a waste of time."

All shop keepers must close their shops 10 minutes before prayer time and shroud the faces of their female mannequins.

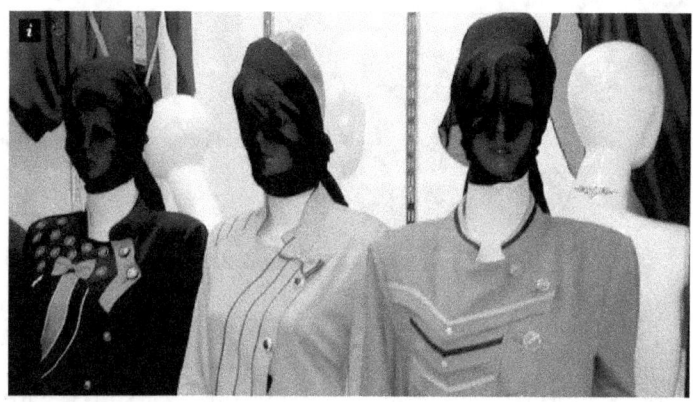

To maintain order, ISIS fighters continuously patrol the streets of the occupied cities, armed to the teeth.

Where do all these guns and tanks and rockets come from?

Most of it from us, ironically – from the good old US of A – when ISIS seized hundreds of millions of dollars of U.S. military equipment after the Iraqi Army had abandoned it following our invasion of their country.

But still, you may ask, occupying great swaths of Syria and Iraq and ruling over 7 million people must cost a fortune, surely?

Indeed it does: two billion dollars to date as a matter of fact, making ISIS the world's richest terrorist organization. So where does all the money come from?

Almost 40% of it comes from the dozens and dozens of oil wells and refineries and pipelines in the north of Iraq and Syria that ISIS has taken over by force...

...involving, among many other things, mass executions of Iraqi oil workers.

Here's a breakdown of ISIS funding sources:

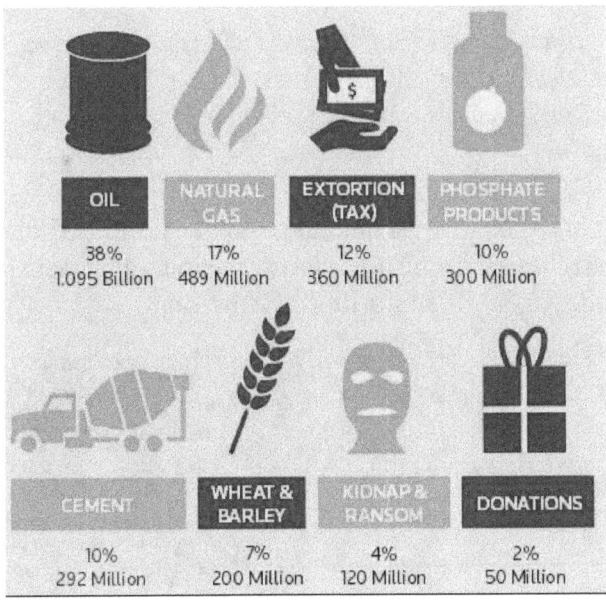

Where did the $50 million's worth of donations come from? Ironically again, from our four greatest Arab friends and allies in the region, plus our Turkish friend and ally:

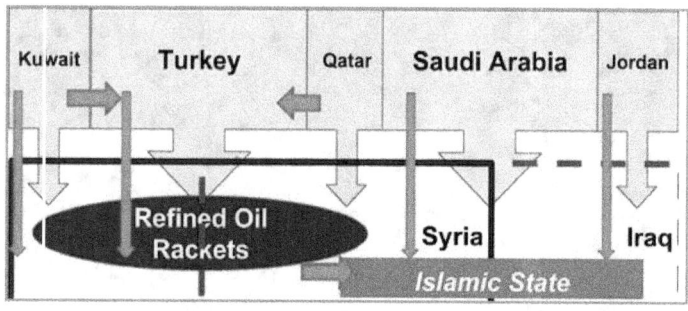

In addition to money, ISIS has also received support and pledges of allegiance from numerous other Islamic terror groups in the following Islamic countries:

*Afghanistan, Algeria, Egypt, India, Indonesia, Iraq, Lebanon, Libya, Mali, Nigeria, Pakistan, Philippines, Saudi Arabia, Sudan, Syria, Tunisia, Uzbekistan and Yemen.*

Note that this list includes Boko Haram, a jihadist group based in northeastern Nigeria, also active in Chad, Niger and in northern Cameroon.

The "Haram" in the name Boko Haram is Arabic for "forbidden" or "sin," and the "Boko" is a word in the Hausa language meaning "fraud" or "inauthenticity," but which is used by these terrorists as a synonym for "Western Education."

There's a catchy bumper sticker slogan for you:

Apart from its worship of the same pseudo-Islamic iron-age claptrap as ISIS, one of Boko Haram's favorite pastimes is kidnapping schoolgirls and doing things to them we don't want to think about.

The leader of this delightful outfit is Abu Bakr Shekau (that name again)...

...who fancies himself the black man's Abu Bakr al-Baghadadi – both of them of course fancying themselves 21st century reincarnations of the original

Abu Bakr, Islam's first caliph, thereby performing the difficult feat achieved by so many of their kind of being simultaneously ludicrous and terrifying.

But we haven't yet mentioned what is perhaps the most terrifying thing of all about ISIS and its partners in crime. Horrific as the beheadings and the crucifixions, and all the rest of it are, what is even more horrific is this:

ISIS is not only bent on destroying hundreds of thousands of Middle Easterners, it is systematically destroying large portions of the cultural heritage not merely of the Arab and ancient Persian world, but of the *entire* world: beginning with the precious Assyrian and Seleucid/Parthian relics of Nimrud, Ninevah and Hatra, part of the 6,000-year-old foundations of all our histories, dating from the dawn of human civilization itself in the Mesopotamian valley.

As ISIS smashes and disfigures the statues in Mosul museum, it tears at the very roots of our shared identity.

The cultural cleansing is complete, the continuity of place and time is lost; the narrative is broken.

ISIS is blowing our past to smithereens.

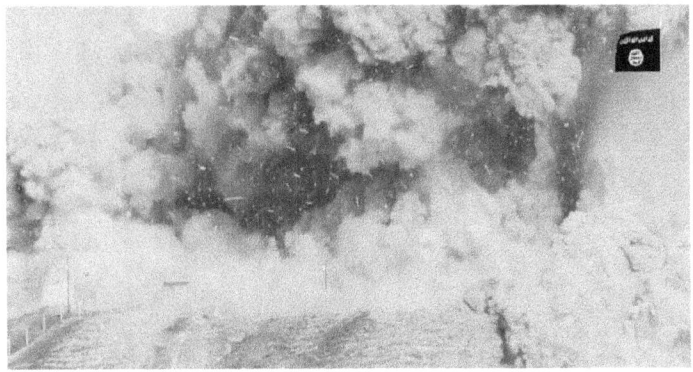

# 8. Propaganda

ISIS wants it both ways: on the one hand, it wants to promote a mythical 7th century way of life at the point of a sword or a spear or a gun or a rocket or a bomb, on the other hand it wants to seduce young and old with every 21st century propaganda technique and medium known to man.

Every day, ISIS posts 90,000 social media messages, texts, blogs and images on the web via FaceBook, Twitter (50,000 accounts), Instagram, Whatsapp, Tumblr, etc., in addition to uploading endless streams of often incredibly violent videos on YouTube:

Every month, ISIS publishes a coffee-table quality online magazine in multiple languages, entitled "Dabiq," the name of a town in northern Syria where ISIS believes the Islamic version of Armageddon will take place when the Muslim and Christian armies eventually face off against each other.

Almost continuously, ISIS produces state-of-the-art video games, inspired by such U.S. productions as "Grand Theft Auto," to recruit the young:

ISIS even employs hip-hop performers, such as the London rapper Abdel-Majed Abdel Bary, to spread its insane, poisonous message:

ISIS also produces an endless stream of online PR videos featuring small children such as these ones in Kazakhstan learning how to assemble high-powered automatic weapons.

No child is too young to learn to kill.

ISIS wants to kill you

ISIS produces Hollywood movies urging *jihad*:

ISIS's most recent propaganda tool to come on line is *al-Bayan* radio network (literally, "The Clearness" or "The Clarion") broadcasting in English, Arabic, French, Russian and Kurdish; the languages of the most fruitful recruiting areas. The date "1434" is from the Islamic Calendar – which begins in 622 A.D. – and is the equivalent of 2013 in our Gregorian Calendar.

Finally, in this litany of loathing, ISIS has trademarked its own iconic symbol: a single raised index finger.

This is a well-known sign of power and victory around the world, but for ISIS, it has a more sinister meaning. It refers to the *tawhid*, the belief in the oneness of God. More specifically, it refers to ISIS's fundamentalist interpretation of the *tawhid*, which rejects any other view, including other Islamic interpretations, as idolatry. It affirms an ideology that demands the destruction of the West and the domination of the world.

The runaway train is gathering steam, soon to be stopping at Israel and Al-Quds, the Holy City, fueled by discontent in the ghettos of Gaza and the West Bank...

...then on to Europe with repeats of scenes such as this...

...and ultimately to its final destination, the lair of the Great Satan Himself...

All this, coming to a theater of war near you...

David Stansfield

...because ISIS will stop at nothing.
Will you?

## 9. How to defeat ISIS

Here are two ways that have been proposed to do this: a left-wing way and a right-wing way. Let's look at these two extremes of the political spectrum.

On the far left, we have Noam Chomsky...

...a world-renowned political dissident, linguist, author of over a hundred books and MIT professor emeritus.

And on the far right, we have Max Boot...

...a military historian and the Jeane J. Kirkpatrick national security senior fellow at the Council on Foreign Relations.

Here is a condensed version of what Noam Chomsky had to say about defeating ISIS on the program, *Democracy Now*, March 3, 2015.

"It's very hard to think of anything serious that can be done. It should be settled diplomatically and peacefully to the extent that that's possible, we should be getting together with (Shi'ite) Iran...

Barak Obama
President of the United

Sayed Ali Khamenei
Supreme Leader of Iran

...which has a huge stake in the matter, and is the main force involved, and with the Iraqi government...

Barak Obama
President of the United

Haider al-Abadi
Prime Minister of Iraq

...which is calling for Iranian support and trying to

work out some arrangement which will satisfy the legitimate demands of the Sunni population, which is what ISIS is protecting and gaining their support from. ISIS is not coming out of nowhere. In Baghdad before the invasion. Sunni and Shia lived intermingled, same neighborhoods, they intermarried, they didn't even know if their neighbor was a Sunni or a Shia. You look at Baghdad today, it's segregated...

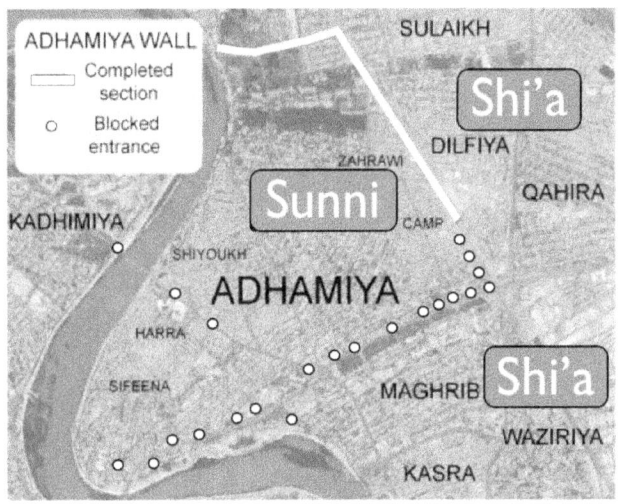

2.5 mile Adhamiya Wall

....a major Sunni-Shia conflict rending the region apart, tearing it to shreds."

"This cannot be dealt with by bombs. This is much more serious than that."

Now for the view from the right.

Here is a condensed version of Max Boot's Council on Foreign Relations Policy Innovation Memorandum No. 51, published November 14, 2014.

"To defeat ISIS, the president needs to dispatch more aircraft, military advisors, and special operations forces...

...and mobilize support from Sunnis in Iraq and Syria, as well as from Turkey, by showing that he is intent on deposing not only ISIS but also the equally murderous regime in Damascus.

"Specific steps include:

- Intensify air strikes.
- Lift the prohibition on U.S. 'boots on the ground.'
- Increase the size of the U.S. force.
- Work with all of Iraq's and Syria's moderate factions.
- Send in the Joint Special Operations Command (JSOC).
- Impose a no-fly zone over part or all of Syria."

What if neither of these plans worked? And nothing in between worked? What might happen if ISIS just continued on its merry way?

We don't know. We can only imagine. It's an extraordinarily complicated situation (in this little book we've only touched on a few of the factors involved). There is no simple answer.

But one thing is clear from all this: ISIS is a cancer that is metastasizing, a virus that is going viral, a plague that is falling on all our houses. Pick your metaphor.

However we describe this ghastly, hyper violent, genocidal organization, ISIS MUST be stopped. We MUST find a solution to this horror.

Could it happen here?

It's already happening here. If only on a very small scale. For now.

Although only a few hundred Americans have been recruited to join ISIS so far, who knows how many of them have already returned home – or will do very shortly?

ISIS wants to kill you

It only takes one.

David Stansfield

The English "interpretations" of the original Arabic of the Koran used throughout this book are by the author's academic adviser at Pembroke College, Cambridge, Professor Arthur John Arberry. See *The Koran Interpreted*, 1955, acknowledged as one of the most prominent English versions by a non-Muslim scholar. The title respects the orthodox Islamic view that the Koran cannot be translated, merely interpreted.

David Stansfield

ISIS wants to kill you

Also by David Stansfield

*Origins: A History of Canada*
*One Last Great Wickedness*
*The Seventh Coming*
*The Man Who Murdered Time*
*Tale Nothing For Granted*
*Blood*
*Got a Couple of Minutes?*
*Attack at Noon*
*Highway Robbery*
*A Season of Monsters*

Contact David Stansfield at:

PO Box 6867
Malibu CA 90264

dstansfield@charter.net

Read my ISIS Blog at:
davidstansfield.wordpress.com

Contact Allen Waldman at:

al@breakoutentertainment.net